The Way
of Abhyasa

The Way of Abhyasa

Meditation in Practice

J. P. Vaswani

BURNS & OATES

First published in Great Britain 1996
BURNS & OATES
Wellwood, North Farm Road,
Tunbridge Wells, Kent TN2 3DR

First published 1995 in the USA
Triumph™ Books
An imprint of Liguori Publications

ISBN 0 86012 266 2

Typeset by Search Press Limited
Printed by BPC Wheatons Ltd, Exeter

*They that set out in search of happiness rarely find it.
But they are truly happy who believe that all that
comes from the hand of God is good!*

CONTENTS

PRACTISE SILENCE, EVERY DAY

We live in a world of deafening noises. Particles of noise cling to our souls: They need to be washed in the waters of silence. Silence cleanses. Silence heals. Silence strengthens.

And silence reveals. Silence will bring you face-to-face with yourself. Who are you? Other people have told you many things about yourself—some complimentary, some otherwise. But all that is not really you. You must now try to find who you are. This is the biggest challenge of life. You must discover yourself. It is not easy to do so—but it can be done!

> Mullah Nasruddin was out in the street
>   searching for something.
> "What are you looking for?"
>   they asked him.
> "I have lost my keys," he answered.
> "Where did you lose them?" he
>   was asked.
> And he said, "I lost them in the house."
> "Then how is it that you are looking for
>   them here?"
> And the Mullah said, "Because in the house
>   it is dark;
> out here it is so bright!"

We have looked for ourselves out here, but we will not be able to find ourselves until we look within, until we turn inside where it is dark.

Every day, preferably at the same time and in the same place—for this is our daily appointment with our own selves, our True Self, the Real Self, the Self Supreme that, for want of a better word, we call God—let us practise silence. Begin with fifteen minutes, then gradually increase the period to at least one hour. At first, the practice may appear to be meaningless, a sheer waste of time. But if you persist in it, silence will become alive and the Word of God will speak to you.

And you will realize that practising silence is, perhaps, the most worthwhile activity of the day.

In silence, let us pray, meditate, repeat the Name Divine, do our spiritual thinking, engage ourselves in a loving and intimate conversation with God.

Prayer is not a complicated affair. It is a very simple matter. It is as simple as talking to a friend. Suppose a friend visited you; it would be natural for you to discuss with that person your ambitions and aspirations, your plans and programmes, your failures and frustrations, and to ask that friend to help you. Do likewise with God.

God is our one true, abiding Friend, the Friend of all friends. And God is available to us at all times. We do not have to go to a particular place to be able to contact God, for God is everywhere. All we have to do is to close our eyes, shut out the world, open our heart, call Him, and there He is in front of us. In the beginning, we will not be able to see Him. Let us be sure that He sees us. In the beginning, we will not be able to hear Him speak. Let us be sure that He hears us. A day will come when we, too, will see Him and hear Him speak.

To be able to see God, we have to put in work. This work is cultivating deep longing for the Lord, deep yearning for the First and Only Fair. As Sri Ramakrishna said: "Long for the Lord even as a lover yearns for his beloved, as a miser yearns for gold, as a child yearns for his mother whom he has lost." Yearn for the Lord. Say to Him with tear-touched eyes: "I need You, Lord! I need nothing else—neither pleasures, nor possessions, nor power! I need You and You alone!" When God gets the assurance that you truly need Him and nothing besides, He will reveal Himself to you.

Think of God in any form that draws you. He is the Formless One, but for the sake of His devotees, He has worn many forms and visited the earth-plane again and again. Call Him by any name that appeals to you. He is the Nameless One, though the sages have called Him by many Names. Do not quarrel over forms or names. You stick to the one that draws you: Let others stick to the ones that draw them. All forms and names ultimately lead to the One Who is beyond form and formlessness. "On whatever path men approach me," says the Lord in the Gita, "on that I go to reach them—for all the paths are Mine, verily Mine!"

So we need to cultivate love—and longing—of the heart. And, therefore, we pray again and again to develop this love for God. Offer set prayers, if you will: But let your prayers emerge out of the very depths of a love-filled heart. "I love You, God! I want to love You more and more! I want to love You more than anything in the world! I want to love You to distraction, intoxication. Grant me pure love and devotion for Your Lotus feet, and so bless me that this world-bewitching *maya*[1] may not lead me astray. And so bless me, Blessed Master, that I may be an instrument of Your help and healing in this world of suffering and pain."

---

1. The negative power: illusion

When a prayer emerges out of the very depths of a love-filled heart, the eyes are touched with tears and the mind does not wander. So many, alas, pray with their lips but their mind is distracted!

It has been truly said that God does not consider the arithmetic of our prayers (how many they are); or the rhetoric of our prayers (how elegant they are); or the music of our prayers (how melodious they are); or the logic of our prayers (how methodical they are); but the sincerity of our prayers—how heartfelt they are.

The idea is to contact God who is the Source of health and happiness and success. Go to the Source if you wish to succeed in life. Make God real to yourself in daily life. Do not let Him be a far-off shadowy Being. Make Him a partner in your daily activities, and you will find miracles happen in your life. And be assured that *there is no problem that God and you cannot solve together. There is no situation that God and you cannot handle together. There is no burden that God and you cannot bear together.*

ALL IS WELL

Prayer does not draw God toward us; it draws us toward God. The more we pray, the more Godlike we become. And we realize that there is nothing that we need. For all is well, all was well and will be well today, tomorrow, and a hundred years hence.

BE STILL AND LISTEN

In prayer we talk to God so much that we fail to hear His Voice. Learn to be still—and you will hear. Until you have heard Him, you have not attained to real communion with Him.

WANDER NOT!

O mind! why do you wander from object to object? Whatever has happened had to happen. Knowing this, do not worry over the past, or be concerned about the future. Cling to the Lotus feet of the Lord and there find true beauty, joy, and peace!

CLOSENESS

In prayer what is essential is not words but the deep silence of communion. When two hearts love, they do not need to speak to each other. They feel happy just being together. In worship, we should feel happy in being close to God. Words, far from being necessary, become futile.

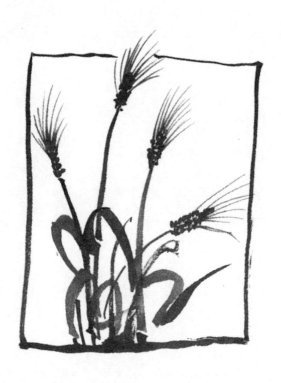

WHAT IS
MEDITATION?

The word "meditation" is derived from the
Latin root that means "to heal."

We live in a world of allurements and entanglements. The sharp arrows of desire, craving, animal appetite, of passion and pride, of ignorance and anger, of hatred and greed, wound our souls, again and again. Our souls bear the scars of many wounds: They need to be healed. Silence is the great healer. We must take a dip every day in the waters of silence if we wish to be healed, cleansed, ennobled, and strengthened for the daily tasks of life.

While many regard meditation as a difficult art, in itself it is so simple. Meditation is directing our attention to eternal things and keeping it there for a while. Within every one of us is a realm of peace, power, perfection. Through practice, we can at will enter this realm and contact God. When we do so, we become conscious of infinite power, a wondrous peace, and realize that everything is perfect and in its own place.

To know what meditation is, we need to go within ourselves and, in the words of Sadhu Vaswani, "sink deeper and deeper." No one else can do that for us: We need to do it ourselves. We need to silence the clamour of our unruly minds; we need to strip ourselves of all pride and passion, selfishness, sensuality, and sluggishness of soul. We need to remove veil after veil until we reach the inmost depths and touch the Pure White Flame.

This first demands that we throw the dirt out of our mind. One is as one thinks, taught the great Rishis of ancient India. Therefore, take care of your thoughts.

"The mind," Bishop Fulton J. Sheen once said, "is like a clock that is constantly running down and must be wound up daily with good thoughts." Fill the mind with noble thoughts. The minds of many, I am afraid, are full of unwholesome thoughts and wrong ideas. It is such thoughts that do not let us live a healthy, happy, and successful life.

Often, we pay scant attention to our thoughts. We say, "After all, it was but a thought." But we must never forget that thoughts are things, thoughts are forces, thoughts are the building blocks of life. With thoughts we are building the edifice of our own life, building our own future. People blame their stars, their destiny. "Men heap together the mistakes of their lives," said John Oliver Hobbes, "and create a monster they call destiny." Destiny is not a matter of chance: it is a matter of choice.

We are building our own destiny, every day, with the thoughts that we think. A thought, if it is constantly held in the mind, will drive us to action. An action that is repeated creates a habit. It is our habits that form our character. And it is character that determines our destiny.

So if we wish to change our destiny, we must begin with a thought. We must change our pattern of thinking. We must cleanse the mind of all the dirt that we have accumulated through the years. Our minds need to be cleansed of thoughts of lust, hatred, greed, passion and pride, selfishness and miserliness, avarice and arrogance, envy and jealousy, resentment and ill will.

Like all spiritual experiences, meditation is something that cannot come to us from without. It is true, in the early stages of our spiritual unfolding, the "exterior" life, in a large measure, does shape the "interior" life. What we think and feel, what we read and hear, what we do and speak, is echoed in the hours of silence. So it is that we must take the greatest care of our "outer" life. We must keep sentinel over our thoughts and feelings, our aspirations and desires, and our words and deeds.

Meditation is gazing inward by opening another aperture of the mind. It is turning away from all outer objects to seek Him whom the Rishis call *Ekamevadvityam*—the One without a second, the one and only Reality. Meditation is entering upon the interior pilgrimage in which layer after layer of unreality is to be torn. The pilgrim, therefore, proceeds by negation: *neti, neti*, not this, not this! These are not God: I seek Him alone!

The pilgrim enters, more and more, into silence. In silence, one understands the secret of true freedom. In silence, one discovers that he or she is not a creature bounded by space and time—but, rather, is a child of Eternity; and Eternity is here and now. He is not the isolated creature he thought himself to be. He is a "wave of the unbounded deep." He is one with all life, all creation. He is in all; all are in Him!

As we sit in silence, let us think of a world that is very much like this world but that is free of all disorder and chaos—a world in which everything is done for love's sake, where everyone readily extends a helping hand to everyone else, where everything comes to pass in the right way, at the right time, in a perfectly harmonious manner. As we do this, we will find the perfection and peace of God flowing into our lives like a perennial river.

In this journey to the Uttermost, it is helpful to have the grace and guidance of a spiritual helper or a friend of God, someone who lives and moves and has his being in God. Such a one we call Teacher, Guru. Such a one is an enlightened one, a man of light and, as Sadhu Vaswani often said, is better than a thousand men who may have read thousands of books. If you would enter into the Secret of Life—the Secret that is God—go and seek someone who is pure and holy and free. Through that one's grace, you will find it easy to tread the Path that the Upanishads have called the "razor's edge."

To grow in the inner life, the life of the Spirit, I need to withdraw from the outer world of noise and excitement. Each day, I must spend some time—at least an hour—in silence. At the very start, perhaps, it will be difficult to sit in silence for an hour at a stretch. Then it would be well if I practice silence for about a quarter of an hour, four times a day.

When sitting in silence, what do I find? I may have selected a silence-corner in a garden or on a riverbank, far from the madding crowd. But, as I go and sit there, I find that I am overwhelmed by a new type of noise. For noise is of two types: exterior and interior. It is easy to keep away from outer noise: There are silence spots in every place, where the din and roar of cities do not reach. But it is a difficult task to still the noise that is within: the clamour of conflicting thoughts.

A beautiful story is told us of Guru Nanak, the Great Master of the Silent Way. A mullah (Muslim priest) meets him and says to him: "You speak of the oneness of all faiths. You urge that the Hindu and the Muslim are both dear to God, whose children are we all. Then come with me and offer worship to Allah in the orthodox Muslim way. Come and do nimaz with me!"

The guru readily consents; and the two go to a mosque. And the priest (the mullah) shows to the prophet (the guru) the way to pray! The mullah inserts his fingers into his ears and kneels down to pray. The mullah goes through the ritual; the guru keeps standing.

Then says the mullah: "Why are you standing there like a log of wood? Why don't you pray with me?"

The guru smiles, then gently says: "My brother, if only you prayed, I, too, would pray with you! But, as your lips uttered the sacred words, your mind, alas! wandered to the stable where your mare is about to give birth to a foal. And you wondered about the colour of its skin. How you wished it were white as wool!"

What am I to do? Do nothing! Let me but sit still, as a silent spectator viewing the shifting scenes of a fickle mind. Let me but sit as, years ago, I sat in a theatre watching a play. The actors appeared on the stage, played their respective roles, then disappeared. I kept looking on! So, too, let me keep looking on at the thoughts that rush out of the unknown deep in a seemingly endless procession. They are not my thoughts. I have naught to do with them. They come; let them come. They will soon pass out, leaving the chamber of my mind cleaner and brighter than before. They are the dirt and filth that have accumulated within the cells of my mind during many years, or, maybe, during a lifetime. If the dirt and filth are washed off, I have every reason to rejoice. The bad odour that is let out in the process should neither frighten me nor disquiet my mind.

In due course, the mind will become calm and clear as the surface of a lake on a windless day. Such a mind will become a source of indescribable joy and peace. Significant are the words of the Upanishad: "The mind alone is the cause of man's bondage; the mind is, also, an instrument of man's liberation."

To sit in silence, I must learn to be still, to do nothing. "The more a man does," says an English mystic, "the more he is and exists. And the more he is and exists, the less of God is and exists within him." To be still, I must learn the art of separating myself from the changing moods of the mind, from its flights, which are faster by far than the fastest supersonic jets.

One simple exercise will be very helpful. Let me imagine the mind in the form of a room. In this room let me select a corner and sweep it clean. Then let me sit in the corner and quietly watch the antics and acrobatics of the mind. If only I can disassociate myself from them, I shall have thrown off the yoke of the mind. I shall have broken the tyranny of the "ego," which is the only hurdle between

me and my God: I shall have grown into that true awareness that, in the midst of my daily duties, keeps my heart
fixed on the One Divine Reality.

Yet another exercise can be very helpful. As I sit in
silence, let me offer my mind flying off on a tangent, and
let me quickly and gently bring it back to the feet of the
Master. If for a whole hour I have done no more than
bring the mind back to the Lord every time it has moved
afar, I have not spent the hour in vain. Gradually, the
mind will be tranquilized and I shall taste and know how
sweet it is to sit in silence.

Sitting in silence, let me repeat the Divine Name or
meditate on some aspect of the Divine Reality or on an
incident in the life of a person of God. God, it is true, is
Nameless: But the sages have called God by many Names.
Choose any Name that appeals to you. Repeat It again and
again, but not merely with the tongue. Repeat It with tears
in the eyes. Repeat It until you can repeat It no longer,
until you disappear from yourself, your "ego" is dissolved,
and you sit in the presence of the Eternal Beloved.

Abu Said was a writer of profane poetry. His poems
were very popular among the lowbrows in old Arabia. One
day, awakening comes to him. Renouncing the path of
popularity, he goes and sits at the feet of a teacher of
spiritual life. And his teacher says to him: "Abu Said! All
the hundred and twenty-four thousand prophets were sent
to preach one word. They bade the people say, 'Allah,' and
devote themselves to Him. Those who heard this Word by
the ear alone let It go by the other ear; but those who heard
It with their souls imprinted It on their souls, and their

24

whole beings became this Word, they became so absorbed in It that they were no more conscious of their own non-existence."

I sometimes think of the Name Divine as a locked door. If only we can open it, we, too, may live in the abiding presence of the Beloved. The way to open it is the Way of Love.

We may also meditate on some form of God, on a saint or a holy One (even though God is the Formless One). Choose any form that draws you and meditate on It. There should, however, be no attachment to the form: all forms, ultimately, have to be left behind. Significant are the words of Meister Eckhart: "He who seeks God under a settled form lays hold of the form, while missing the God concealed in it." Meditate on the form to which you feel drawn; then go beyond it. Enter into the form to meet the Formless One!

The Buddha speaks of five types of meditation. The first is the *meditation of love*, in which we so adjust our heart that we wish for the happiness of all living things, including the happiness of our enemies.

The second is the *meditation of compassion*, in which we think of all beings in distress, vividly representing in our imagination their sorrows and anxieties so as to arouse a deep compassion for them within us.

The third is the *meditation of joy*, in which we think of the prosperity of others and rejoice with their rejoicings.

The fourth is the *meditation on impurity*, in which we think of the evil consequences of immorality and corruption. In this meditation, we realize how trivial is the pleasure of the moment and how fatal are its consequences!

The fifth is the *meditation on serenity*, in which we rise above love and hate, tyranny and oppression, wealth and want, and regard our own fate with impartial calm and perfect tranquillity.

The life of meditation must be blended with the life of work. For we must not give up our worldly duties and obligations in order to meditate. We must withdraw ourselves from the world for a while and give ourselves wholly to God. Then we must return to our daily work, pouring into it the energy of the Spirit. Such work will bless the world. Through such work will God Himself descend upon the earth. Work of the true type is a bridge between God and humanity. So, with one hand let us cling to His Lotus feet and with the other attend to our daily duties.

The problem, then, is how do I remember God even in the midst of multifarious activities? If, while praying, we can think of worldly matters, why can we not, while doing worldly work, think of God?

1. *Be Still!* From time to time, as often as I can, in the midst of daily work, of tumult and tempest, let me pause for a brief moment and lift up my heart in loving converse with God. Let me speak to Him as I speak to my dear mother or to a loving friend. My words must not have

been carefully prepared, nor should they necessarily be quotations from the Scriptures. What I speak to God must flow naturally and spontaneously out of the purity and simplicity of my heart. One day, as Sadhu Vaswani lay on his bed of sickness, there were the following words on his lips:

> My heart, O Lord, is thirsty for Thy Light
> and Thy Love!
> Come to me each day, in my thoughts
> and aspirations.
> Come to me in my dreams, in the laughter on
> my lips, in the tears in my eyes.
> In my worship and my work, in life and in
> death, come Thou to me.
> Be Thou with me in Thy Mercy and Thy
> Love!

In moments of trial and temptation, let me call out to God: "Help me, O Helper of the helpless ones!" Even when my foot has slipped, let me hold out my arms and cry: "Lord, lift me up!" While attending to my common duties, let me ask God to be by me, to be with me, so that every little act may become a communion with Him who has no need of words but who is only too eager to accept the offering of love.

Bring the heart back to the sweet, familiar presence of God. Be still and let the Peace of God flow into you! It is only when the soul is at peace that true work is done, and the body and mind have the strength to bear and endure.

2. *Be Calm!* Let me do nothing that may disturb my peace of mind and heart. Let my daily life be so regulated as to strengthen the inner calm, not take away from it. So let me avoid overwork. And let me not be in a hurry to do anything. Let me go about my work quietly, gently, and lovingly, my mind and heart devoted to the Lotus feet of the Lord. Then will my soul become strong and all around me the world will smile.

3. *Seek God!* In the midst of my work—aye, even in the midst of my kirtan and worship—let me, again and again, withdraw for a brief while into the inner chamber of my heart and there speak to God, gaze upon His beauteous face, touch the hem of His garment, cling to His Lotus · feet. Let me do this from time to time throughout the day and night. Truly blessed are these brief moments of intimate contact with God, when I penetrate into the very depths of my soul and offer all I have and all I am to Him and feel grateful to Him for His everlasting mercy and loving tenderness.

This may not be accomplished within a day, a week, or a month. But nothing is impossible to anyone who, in faith and devotion, treads the Way of *Abhyasa*, the Path of Practice. Is it not declared in the Gita:

> However difficult or impossible
> it may seem,
> You, O Arjuna! may still achieve it.
> By steadfast effort and wholehearted
> devotion.
> So walk the Way of Practice!

And as the Chinese say: "The journey of a thousand miles begins with one step." We may be far, very far, from the goal. But even if we have taken a single step in the right direction, we have advanced on the Path. And for every single step that we take to reach God, God takes a hundred steps to draw nearer to us. For, while we think we are seeking God, in reality it is God who is in search of us.

WHAT JESUS SAID

This day, I meditated a little on the threefold teaching of the Master to His dear disciple Peter as they were sailing in a boat. In this teaching of Jesus is summed up the secret of the practice of silence and meditation.

(1) "Peter, thrust out a little from the land!" *That is, be not of the earth, earthy. Be detached. Let not the earth—its pleasures and possessions and power—hold you captive. Leave the earth for a while, and know that you are a child of the Spirit.*

(2) "Launch out into the deep!" *That is, enter into the depths within you. In the depths within is He, Thy Master and Thy Lord. Enter into the depths and consider His Love, His Wisdom, His Strength, His Joy, and His Peace. In the depths within, be alone with the Alone, and let His Love and Compassion fill your entire being.*

(3)   "Let down your nets for a catch!" *That is, open your hearts to receive the rich treasures that the Lord gives in abundance to whoever ventures into the depths within to meet Him. Receive—and then come and spend time in the service of those who suffer and are in pain. Be a channel of God's Mercy to a broken world!*

How Do I Proceed?

The following are only a few "guidelines" and need not be strictly adhered to. Meditation is a most "personal" experience in that it involves one's deepest and truest self.

Every person meditates in his or her own way, for the "Spirit blows where it wills." The one who treads the path of meditation becomes a pilgrim of the Spirit, always on the move, always eager to sink deeper and deeper within himself, until he loses himself in the Pure White Light. The following, therefore, are only a few practical suggestions.

1. Select a silence-corner or a silence-chamber where you can spend some time every day without being disturbed. It should preferably be away from the telephone and should be dimly lighted.

2. It is advisable to get up as early as possible in the morning, in any case before sunrise. The period of three hours before sunrise is known as *Brahma-mahoorat*, and is especially favorable for meditation. At that time, the atmosphere is calm and serene, the body is fresh and rested, the mind is alert but not overactive. The hour of evening twilight is also good for meditation.

   If, however, these hours are not found convenient, any other suitable time may be fixed.

3. If, at the time of meditation, you feel drowsy, there is no harm if you have a cup of tea or coffee or if you walk up and down for some time or do a light exercise.

4. Meditation should be practised preferably at the same time and the same place, every day. This will help form a habit that will automatically throw you into a meditative

mood when the hour approaches.

5. Meditation should be practised when the body is not tired and at least two hours after having a meal.

6. At the time of meditation, it is helpful to wear loose, comfortable clothes. This will help you to relax fully. The clothes should be clean and, if possible, set apart for this purpose.

7. No particular posture is prescribed for meditation. Adopt any sitting posture that you find natural and in which you can sit steadily for some length of time without having to move the body unnecessarily. You may sit on the floor (not on the bare ground but on a mat, a carpet, or a piece of cloth) in a cross-legged position or be in a straight chair with your feet gently resting on the floor. What is important is that the spinal column and the head should be held erect. This helps the *prana* (vital energy) to move freely in the body. Do not strain. Be comfortable, relaxed, and attentive.

8. If, in the course of meditation, you feel cramps or pain or get an itching sensation in any part of the body, do not move but concentrate on the part where you feel the pain (or itch or any other sensation) and mentally repeat the word *pain ... pain ... pain ...* (or *itch ... itch ... itch ...* and so on) over and over again, and the pain will disappear and you can continue your practice of meditation.

If, however, at any time you find that the pain is

intolerable, you may change the position without disturbing the erect position of the body.

9. It helps to wear a soft smile on the face. This aids in brightening the mind and makes it happier.

10. Relax. Take a few deep breaths. Also take God's Name a few times in such a way that its resonance is mentally heard. Turn the mind either inward or upward. There are three centres on which you may fix the attention of the mind: (a) the heart (not the physical heart but what is called the "spiritual heart"—it is in the middle of the chest, in line with the physical heart); (b) the point between (and a little behind) the two eyebrows; and (c) the head. Choose the centre where the consciousness easily and naturally settles down.

11. You do not have to concentrate or to meditate upon these positions. You have only to station yourself in your consciousness at one of these centres and be there for the duration of the meditation.

The meditation may then begin

(A few methods of meditation are given at the close of this chapter, although there are many, many more. Choose the one that suits you.)

12. As you try to concentrate, you will find that, in the early stages, untoward thoughts will make your attention

wander. This is natural. The mind has the habit of wandering: It must wander. You will be annoyed at how many and how trivial these distractions can be. But you must deal with them kindly. Do not drive them out in anger. Be gentle with them. Label each distraction as past-present-future-worthy-unworthy-jealousy-envy-hatred-vanity-desire-egotism, and so on. As you label them, they will slink away and leave you in peace. Once they disappear, your attention will return to meditation.

13. If, during the meditation, you see any lights or figures or images (or hear sounds or notice a fragrance), observe them in a detached manner. Do not feel elated; do not shut them out. They are generally signs of the opening of the subtler senses of sight or sound or smell. Some people have such experiences; others do not. Experiences, by themselves, may mean nothing. What is important is attaining to purity, peace, love, compassion, joy. What is important is the transformation of one's life.

14. After meditation, do not immediately plunge into active work. Be quiet for some time and gently move out of the world of silence into the world of activity.

15. You must carry the spirit of meditation into the workaday world. The peace and purity you have experienced in periods of silence must be reflected in your dealings with others. Emotions like hatred, anger, resentment, ill will, greed, arrogance, self-love, covetousness, envy, jealousy, agitation, anxiety, must be transcended.

Suggested Methods

1. Concentrate on a mantra, a holy Name, a word or syllable, which to you is symbolic of God or Truth (the shorter the mantra, the better). Repeat It again and again. Repeat It in a musical manner. Repeat It with deep love and longing of the heart. Repeat It until It gets fixed in your mind and is in the background of your consciousness all the time, even while you are working or are asleep.

Any mantra or holy Name or word or syllable that draws you may be taken up. There is, for example, the ancient mantra "*Om*" or "*Raam*." Other mantras include: "*Om Bhagavate Vaasudevaaya*"; "*Om Namaha Sivaaya*"; "*Om, Sri Raam, Jaya Raam, Jaya Jaya Raam*"; "*Om Mani Padme Hum*"; "Jesus"; "Lord Jesus Christ, have mercy on me"; "Yehovah." The list is endless.

2. Concentrate on an object or form that to you is symbolic of God or Truth. In the initial stages, you may take up a picture of that One and place it in front of you at eye level. Gaze steadily at the picture and, after some time, close your eyes and fix the picture at the centre of concentration. Do this in a relaxed manner, without strain. After some time, the mental vision will fade away. Open your eyes again and steadily gaze at the picture. Repeat the process a number of times. A stage will come when you will be able to visualize the picture wherever you are.

3. Blend methods 1 and 2. Concentrate on the form, and, at the same time, keep on repeating the Name Divine. You will find this practice very rewarding.

4. Concentrate on an incident from the life of your Master—Krishna, Buddha, Jesus, and so on. Let your mind revolve around the incident. Say to yourself (mentally), *The Master was so patient. He was so loving, forgiving ....* *When shall I be likewise?* Through concentration on such incidents, you will sink deeper and deeper within yourself.

5. Concentrate on a subtle object: an idea, an aspiration, a quality such as love, joy, peace, humility, compassion, tranquillity....

6. Do not concentrate directly on God (the Supreme Being), but concentrate on God existing in the heart of your guru and on whom the guru himself is meditating with unflinching devotion and perfect concentration. The guru may be a living person or, better still, a Great One who has passed on: a saint, a prophet, a person of God. Have a mental picture of the guru in the act and posture of deep meditation and, as you meditate on the object of his meditation, you will be richly rewarded.

7. Concentrate on a "saying" or an "utterance" of a Great One, or a *sloka*, a line from a Scripture that is dear to you. (A few thoughts for meditation are given on page 81.) Repeat the words a number of times. Let the mind revolve around the words. Enter into the depths of meaning that

are contained in the words. This will produce a train of thoughts centring around the "saying" or "utterance." A stage will come when thoughts will vanish, and you will have gone beyond the "mind."

8. Concentrate on your breathing. Feel the air come in at the tip of the nostrils as you inhale. Feel the air flow out at the tip of the nostrils as you exhale. Do not follow the breath as it enters the lungs. Do not control your breathing. Do not attempt to deepen it. This is not an exercise in breathing. Do not interfere with your breathing. Only feel the air at the tip of the nostrils, as it comes in and flows out. You will find that your attention will wander, again and again. All you have to do is gently bring back your attention to the process. Do not struggle with thoughts or feelings. Gently bring back your attention to your breath. It will grow quieter and quieter. It will slow down to a point of almost indistinguishable rhythm. You must not tense your muscles. Non-effort is the key to success in meditation.

As you practice this meditation, you will gradually find, in the words of a great teacher, that "your breathing is your greatest friend. Return to it in all your troubles and you will find comfort and guidance."

9. As you sit to meditate, turn your attention inward, observe the natural breathing cycle, and with inhalation listen to the sound of one part of a mantra and with exhalation listen to the other part of the mantra. For instance, if your mantra is *Om Raam*, with inhalation listen

40

to the sound of "*Om*," with exhalation listen to the sound of "*Raam.*" If your mantra is *Soham*, with inhalation listen to the sound of "*So*," with exhalation listen to the sound of "*ham.*" You do not have to utter the mantra mentally. You have to listen to the sound in your mind.

10. Keep a lighted candle (with a sufficiently strong flame) at eye level, say at a distance of about fifteen inches. Take a deep breath and mentally say to yourself: *I am surrounded by the loving Light of the Spirit.* Continue to gaze steadily at the flame for some time, keeping blinking to a minimum. Then close your eyes and pay attention to the image of the flame at the point between the two eyebrows. Gradually the image will fade away. Open your eyes and repeat the procedure (that is, gaze steadily at the flame, and so on). You may repeat this practice a few times.

11. This is a meditation of six steps, each of which takes roughly two and a half minutes.

The first is the step of *rhythmic breathing*. Breathe in slowly, easily, evenly, and deeply, and then breathe out slowly, easily, evenly, and deeply. Within two minutes and a half you will be able to breathe in (and out) fifteen times. As your breathing becomes rhythmic, your tensions will relax. If you like, you may blend the repetition of the Name with your breathing.

The second is the step of *detached observation*. As an observer, watch the movements of the mind. Do not involve yourself with the mind. You are not the mind; the mind is not yours. You are only a silent observer. Observe without judgment.

The third is the step of *serenity, peace*. You are like a rock in the midst of an ocean. Waves (distracting thoughts) arise; they come and dash against the rock. The rock is unaffected, calm, tranquil.

The fourth is the step where you realize your *oneness* with all that is: all people, all creatures, all things, all conditions. You are not apart from others. The others and you are but parts of the One Great Whole. You are in every person, in every bird and animal, in every fowl and fish, in every insect, in every shrub and plant. You belong to all countries and communities, all races and religions. You are at one with the universe. (This type of meditation will fill your heart with loving-kindness, so much so that, in due course, you will find it difficult to snuff out the life of even a small insect.)

You are not merely in your physical body: You are in all that is. If the body drops down, you will continue to be. You will be in every grain of sand, in every drop of water, in every ray of sunshine. Death cannot touch you. You are immortal.

The fifth step is meditation on your *immortality*. If you are at one with all humanity, then even if there is but one human being alive, you are alive. If you are at one with all living creatures, then even if there is but one creature breathing the breath of life, you are alive. If you are at one with trees and flowers, then even if there is but one leaf fluttering in the wind, you are alive. Yes—you are immortal, eternal, deathless.

The sixth step is *breathing out peace and happiness and*

goodwill to all. You are in all. Therefore, it is natural for you to breathe out peace and happiness and goodwill to all. May all be happy and full of bliss. Think of all who dwell in Northern lands ... Southern lands ... Eastern lands— Western lands. Breathe out peace and goodwill to all. May all be happy and full of bliss. All living things, whether they be near or far, tall or short, rich or poor, educated or illiterate, whether they be born or are still in the womb, may all be happy and full of bliss. May those that love you and those that, for some reason or other, are unable to love you; may those that speak well of you and those that, for some reason or other, are unable to speak well of you— may all, all, without exception—be happy and full of bliss. You are in them all. It is only when they become happy that you are happy. May all be free from disease, free from ignorance, free from sorrow!

As you get up from this meditation, you will feel that you yourself are happy and full of bliss.

There are many other methods. Choose the one you like and be regular in your practice. In the beginning, there will be days when the practice will be dry, boring, tiresome. Do not, on that account, give up the practice. New grooves are to be cut. Through a process of many births, the mind has acquired the habit of wandering. And it will take some time for this wandering to cease.

After some months of repeated and regular practice, you will arrive at a stage where you will be filled with indescribable joy and happiness. This is known as the "bliss of concentration." Those who have tasted it but once miss it greatly if perchance, one day, due to overwork or otherwise, they are unable to sit in silence.

Many today are turning to meditation to reduce the effects of stress and anxiety, to grow in awareness, to improve their health or emotional stability. They achieve the results they are looking for. But it must not be forgotten that the true goal of meditation is God. Meditation should aim at detaching the heart from all that is not-God, and at giving to it, as its sole occupation, communion with the Divine Being. Therefore, even in the midst of your daily work, pause for a while and breathe out an aspiration such as "I love you, God! I want to love You more and more!"

Where there is love, meditation becomes easy and natural.

THE WAY OF LOVE

Within the heart
is enshrined
The Secret of Nama—
The Name Divine.

The way to unlock the Secret
Is the Way of love.
Teach me, O Lord,

To love Thee,
Not myself!

So bless me that, forsaking myself
I may meditate on Thy Lotus feet,
By day and by night!

THE NAME DIVINE

Doing *japa* (repetition of the Divine Name) mechanically is better than not doing it at all.

But even better than doing it mechanically is to do it with an intense feeling of love for the Lord.

Utter the Name as though you are calling the Beloved. What a thrill this should give you! Your hair should stand on end, your eyes should become pools of tears, your mind should be concentrated on the beauteous face of the Beloved!

This is not possible without the grace of God.

Let us cry for God's grace.

God is our mother. If we keep on crying, she will not keep away from us for long!

RELAX! RELAX! RELAX!

M editation begins with relaxation. Most of the time we are tense without realizing it. Even when we go to sleep, our body and mind are not relaxed: We carry the tensions of the day with us and so do not have restful sleep. We wake up the next morning

with a feeling of languor or fatigue. We do not feel fresh and strong to meet the challenges of the new day. This goes on day after day, and the tension keeps on accumulating, until it manifests itself in one physical illness or another. So many diseases of the present day—heart attack, high blood pressure, nervous breakdown, migraine headache, asthma—are due to the build-up of tension. It has been rightly said that "people do not die of disease: they die of internal combustion." The demand for tranquilizers increases day by day. What is needed is to relax—if possible, twice every day.

There are many methods of relaxation; each person must follow the one that best suits him or her. Here is a simple, easy eleven-step method:

1. Lie on your back on the floor (or a carpet). Or sit on the floor in a comfortable posture. Or in a chair with your feet gently touching the floor. Take a few deep breaths, exhaling each slowly, completely emptying the lungs.

2. Imagine yourself in the loving, immediate, and personal presence of the Lord (your Beloved). You are sitting at His Lotus feet with your arms girdling His ankles, your head resting on His feet. Say to yourself: "Here is true rest. Here is true relaxation. In Thy presence, fears and frustrations, worries and anxieties, depressions and disappointments, tensions and tribulations, vanish as mist before the rising sun. I am relaxed. Relax … relax … relax."

3. To relax a muscle, you must first tighten it, then let it

go. As you let it go, it may perhaps help you to utter the words: "Let go, let go, let God!"

4. Turn your attention to the muscles around the eyes. Relax-relax-relax. Open the eyes and imagine that the eyelids have become heavy. Let them drop on the eyes. Lift them and let them shut three times.

5. Move on to the muscles around the mouth. Tighten them and let go. Relax-relax-relax.

6. Relax your facial muscles. Clench your teeth, then relax, letting your face go limp. Relax-relax-relax.

7. Repeat the process throughout the body: neck, right shoulder, elbow, forearm, wrist, hand, fingers, left shoulder, elbow, forearm, wrist, hand, fingers, back, chest, abdomen, buttocks, calves, ankles, feet, toes. Push your toes down toward the carpet, stretch and relax. Pull your feet up toward the legs, stretch and relax. Relax-relax-relax.

8. Breathe in and stretch your whole body, relax, and exhale. Repeat this three times. Relax-relax-relax. You are calm, relaxed, peaceful, serene. You are resting at the Lotus feet of the Lord—calm, relaxed, peaceful, serene.

9. You are now lighter than air, moving upward, upward, floating as a cloud—calm, relaxed, peaceful, serene.

10. You are in the presence of the Lord. Offer this simple

prayer: "Thou art by me, a living and radiant Presence, and I am relaxed, calm, peaceful, serene." Repeat the prayer a few times. You are now completely relaxed.

11. When you wish to close this exercise in relaxation, rub the palms of your hands together, place them gently on the eyelids, and gently open the eyes.

THE GUIDING VOICE

When your heart is troubled, try to enter within. Within everyone is the Sanctuary of the Soul, a Holy Place, a Divine Centre, a Guiding Voice, which we can hear when we are still.

Forget the meaningless things that are happening in the outer world—forget, forgive, give over, be free!

REST IN HIM

Be not anxious to do God's work.

He is the One Worker; let Him work in and through you, if and when it be His Will.

So be still as the lute is still; and let the Master-Musician strike what music He will out of your life.

Rest in Him; and let every breath that you draw be an offering to Him.

A Simple
Exercise

Our lives need to be renewed, if possible, daily—through contact with God. The rain of God's mercy pours every day; and those of us who receive it are washed clean, renewed and re-strengthened for the struggle of life, as servants of God.

May I suggest to you a simple exercise? Every morning, as you sit in silence, close your eyes and imagine the Life of God coursing through every part of your body, filling it through and through. The Life of God is in us already: We have to be conscious of it. Say to yourself: *Every moment the Life of God*—call Him by what Name you will; they are all so many names of Him who is Nameless—*is filling every nerve and cell and fibre of my being!*

Then begin with the head. Feel the Life of God coursing through your head, and say: "The Life of God is renewing, revitalizing my entire brain, every nerve and nerve centre, and the entire cerebro-spinal system. And my brain thinks the thoughts of God. It thinks in obedience to the Moral Law...

"The Life of God is renewing the entire sensory system. It is revitalizing the eyes; and now my eyes see more clearly, more purely. God's Light shines in and through them: And the Light of God is the light of purity....

"God's Life is revitalizing my ears. They hear more clearly and they hear words that are good and noble; and they hear the music of God that thrills the universe from end to end....

"God's Life is revitalizing my nose.... God's Life is revitalizing my throat. How sweetly it sings the Name of God and the songs of the saints of God! And it utters words that are sweet and true and helpful to humanity!"

Now pause for a moment. Then take in a deep breath and turn your attention to the lungs and the heart. Imagine the Life of God renewing, revitalizing, the chest and the heart. The heart is the seat of emotions, and because God's

Life is in it, I shall be emotionally balanced, calm and serene in every situation and circumstance of life.

Turn your attention to your arms and hands. They are the hands of God. They are instruments of God's help and healing in this world of suffering and pain.... Think of the stomach and other organs.... Then come to your legs, knees, and feet. The feet are now firmly set on the path of righteousness and self-realization.

After covering your entire body, concentrate once again on the heart. The heart is the Sanctuary of the Temple, the Abode of the Lord. And now imagine the Lord seated in the heart—for that is where He is already—His Love, His Wisdom, His Strength, His Intelligence, His Joy, His Peace, all centred there and reaching out to every part of your body and outside to your dear and near ones, and to your friends and "foes" alike.

It will take you longer to read this than to put this simple exercise into practice. Repeat this exercise, as often as you can, during the day. But do it at least twice every day—in the morning and at night. And you will soon, very soon, see the effects of it. Your health will improve. Your mind will be more relaxed and alert. Your heart will be more respon-sive to the pain of others. And you will grow into a fuller, richer, deeper consciousness of the presence of God. He will be more real to you than the things of this earth. New love and longing for Him will wake up within your heart. And you will aspire to dedicate all you are, and all you have, at His Lotus feet for the service of suffering creation. You will live and move and have your being in the Joy and Peace of God. You will be blessed among all the children of the world.

ENTER WITHIN

The Kingdom of Heaven is seeking every one of us.

"Come unto Me!" It says to every pilgrim on the Path.

To be able to enter the Kingdom, all we have to do is to get to the center, leaving on the circumference everything that keeps us moving on the circumference.

THE DEDICATED LIFE

Seek to love God not with the intellect but with all your heart.

Make your heart empty of everything, and the Lord will fill it with His Love.

Let the heart be wholly reserved for Him; let it move out to none else.

Our hearts keep on wandering—sometimes after this form, sometimes after that object.

This wandering will not cease until the heart has found its focus; and the focus is God.

So it is that the Christian mystic Saint Augustine said:

"Our hearts are restless until they rest in Thee!"

When this happens, not merely the heart but also the mind and body—the entire person—becomes an offering at His Lotus feet. This is what is meant by the dedicated life.

GUIDED
MEDITATIONS

Guided meditation sessions form an integral part of the programmes at Sadhana camps (spiritual camps), held in both Eastern and Western lands. Retreatants meet together in a hall and are guided, step by step, with the help of audiotapes.

The following few examples, adapted for this book, have been used with good results; perhaps they will help you.

Awareness Meditation

This meditation calms the restless and agitated mind and helps in increasing the power to concentrate on work, studies, and spiritual development. But it is not as simple as it may seem on the surface.

Let us relax. One of the main obstacles on the path of meditation is physical tension. There are many who believe that meditation is only a means; that the end is relaxation. Actually, it is the other way around: Relaxation is the means; meditation is the goal. Try to relax every muscle, every nerve, every limb, of the body—make the body tension-free. Relax the mind as well; let it be free of fear, anxiety, frustration, worry, depression, disappointment. Even as a towel is wrung to drain it of every drop of water, so let the mind, pictured in the form of a towel, be drained of all tension, drop by drop.

We are now ready to embark on a spiritual journey that, under God's grace, will take us into the depths within and give us that which surpasses understanding. (Now follow the steps and exercises outlined on pages 50 to 52 for comfortable posturing, breathing awareness, and using mantras).

As I've mentioned before, in the beginning of such exercises you will find your attention often wanders. The Cistercian monk Thomas Keating describes this wandering as "woolgathering" and says it is caused by the imagination's "propensity for perpetual motion." For some time, you may not even be conscious of the wandering. But as soon as you do become aware, gently bring back your attention to your breath, as it enters and leaves the nostrils.

You will be amazed at how many and how trivial these wanderings can be. The mind keeps jumping from one place to another, from one object to another. Hopes, fears, and memories pass through the mind in seemingly endless procession. We do not have to fight the mind. In fact, we cannot fight the mind; it can be a very powerful adversary. We have to humour it. We have to bring the mind back, gently and lovingly, to our breathing.

As we breathe, let us actually *feel* the air coming in and flowing out our nostrils. Keep all attention on the tip of the nostrils.

Remain silent for about three minutes.

The attention has wandered from the tip of the nostrils. Gently, very gently, bring it back to the breathing. Be alert!

Remain silent for about three minutes.

Be relaxed and let the face wear a soft smile.

Remain silent for about three minutes.

Do not interfere with the breathing; merely watch it. Watch the breath as it comes in and flows out at the tip of the nostrils.

Remain silent for about three minutes.

This is an exercise in awareness. We do not have to control the breath; we have only to watch it. Be relaxed and let the face wear a soft smile. And be alert!

Remain silent for five minutes.

You have now meditated for seventeen minutes. The period of silence is over. Rub the palms of your hands together, softly place them on your eyelids, and gently open your eyes. *Om, shanti, shanti, shanti!*

Death Meditation

Let us, for a short while, forget the world—its worries and woes, problems and perplexities—and feel that we are in the loving, the immediate, the personal presence of God. God is not far from us. He is wherever we are. He is here, He is now. All we have to do is close our eyes, shut out the world, open our heart, and call Him. And He is here in front of us!

Let us begin this meditation with a short prayer:

Lord, I need You! I love You!
I want to love You more than anything
   in the world!
I want to love You so that I may be lost in
   You completely!
Grant me pure love and devotion for
   Your Lotus feet,
   and so bless me that this world-bewitching
   maya may not lead me astray.
And make me, Blessed Master, an instrument of
   Your help and healing in the world of
   suffering and pain!

Now let us relax. Relax every muscle, every limb, every nerve in the body. Make it tension-free. If you like, you may mentally picture the body in the form of a huge sack of potatoes. The sack is cut at the middle, allowing the potatoes to roll out. How relaxed is the empty sack! Let the body feel relaxed likewise.

Now let the mind be free of worries of the past and fears or expectations of the future. Let us live in the present— the here and the now!

Now let us sit in a comfortable posture, so that we will not need to change it, for a period of about twenty-five to thirty minutes. Let us sit comfortably, preferably in a cross-legged position, and keep our spine erect. Or you can sit in a chair, keeping your spine erect and your feet gently touching the floor.

Now take in three deep breaths. As you breathe deeply, be relaxed. Begin. Breathe in slowly, deeply ... (*pause*).

Now exhale slowly, completely ... (*pause*).

Now blend your breathing with the repetition of the sacred syllable "*Om*." First, fill your lungs quickly; then, as you slowly let out the breath, utter the sacred word "*Om*." One-third of the utterance should be with parted lips, and the remaining two-thirds with lips closed. This will create a vibration within you. Do this three times. Take in the breath quickly, then slowly let out the breath and utter "*Om*."

> *Om* ...
> *Om* ...
> *Om* ...

Now let us meditate a little on the transitoriness of life. No one can stay on earth forever, but so many, alas, live in mortal fear of death. So many are afraid of death. We forget that birth and death are but two sides of the same coin. Wherever there is birth, there is bound to be death. Whoever is born must die. Leaving the body is called death, even as entering the body is called birth. Death applies only to the physical body. When the body drops down, when the body dies, we do not die. We are immortal, eternal, deathless. It is the body that dies.

As the Lord Sri Krishna says in the *Bhagavad Gita*, the body is only a garment that we have worn. The garment drops down, the garment becomes useless, but the wearer of the garment continues to live. From now on, never say that you will die. It is the physical body that dies. The *jiv-atman*—the soul that wears the physical body—continues to live in the life that is undying. Once you understand this, you will never be afraid of death. The root cause of our fear is our identification with the physical body. We have identified ourselves with our physical bodies. The physical body is only a house in which we dwell for a brief while. The house crumbles; the tenant of the house continues to live. He lives in some other house.

Now let us consider a little of the experience through which a person passes when the physical body dies. In the moment of death, God will appear to us in the form in which we have thought of Him. In the moment of death, that form of light will appear to us and, with tender, love-filled eyes, will look at us and will put to us the question: "My child! What have you done with your life?" In that moment, we will realize that life was given to us as a gift from God for a special purpose. Alas, lured by temptations, entangled by desire, pulled by passion, we completely forgot this purpose. We squandered our life, we chased shadow-shapes that came and went. We ran after pleasures and possessions and power and, in the process, turned away, again and again, from the Light. We bartered the precious thing called life for transitory joys and ephemeral possessions. We earned nothing. And now we stand in the presence of God, empty-handed. What answer may we give to His question: "My child! What have you done with your life?"

There is comfort in the thought that it is not yet too late. So long as there is breath in this body, so long do we have the opportunity to fulfill the purpose for which we have been sent to the earth-plane. Therefore, let us spend some time in silence and ask ourselves the questions: "Who am I? What is the purpose of my visit to the earth-plane? Where am I moving? Am I drifting away or am I drawing nearer to the goal?" When we set out on a long journey, we take along money and provisions. When we have to appear for an examination, we first study hard to be able to show brilliant results. The journey of death, the inevitable journey that none of us can avoid, is the greatest journey we shall ever undertake. Shall we set out on the journey empty-handed?

Sant Gyaneshwar says: "As long as you can speak, let your words be kind! Before the hands become paralyzed, let us keep on giving as much as we can! As long as the mind can work, let us think pure, noble, holy thoughts! And, above all, let us arrange our house while the lamp is yet burning!" Soon the night comes, when no one can work. Let every day of our life be a day of preparation. *Prepare! Prepare!* This is the one word that our dear ones on the Other Side wish to pass on to us. *Prepare! Prepare!* For they find us chasing things that, to them, are no better than shadows. They find us running after money, trying to gather millions, not a single penny of which we will be allowed to carry with us into the Great Beyond. They find us running after pleasures and sense-enjoyments—after name, fame, greatness, and earthly glory. These are all shadows. So they ask us to open our eyes, to wake up from the slumber of the senses and the mind, and prepare for the inevitable journey, the journey that awaits us.

How do we prepare?

1. Let us establish a link of love and devotion with someone who, to us, is a symbol of Truth or God. Let us
establish a link of love and devotion with God Himself.
Every day, let us strengthen this link of love and devotion.
Every day, let us pray to Him, let us kiss His holy feet, let
us offer all our work to Him, let us, in moments of silence,
converse with Him, in love and with intimacy. Let this link
grow, from more to still more, until we feel that, wherever
we are, we are not far from Him. We are overshadowed by
His radiant presence. And in His presence there can be no
death. For when this body drops down, He will be by us,
and He will lift us in His loving, everlasting arms, and He
will lead us on—ever onward, forward, Godward.

2. As we establish this link of love and devotion with God,
we shall realize that in everything that happens, there is a
meaning of God's mercy. Many things happen in life: we
are unable to understand the "why" of them. Suddenly our
dear ones are snatched away from us, suddenly a misfortune overtakes us. Instead of wasting our time and energy
in inquiring why such a bitter experience entered our life,
let us move forward to greet every incident and accident,
every illness and adversity, every misfortune and calamity,
with the words: "I accept! I accept!"

3. Be a blessing to others. In the measure in which you
become unselfish, in that measure your heart expands.
Those who lead selfish lives on earth, those who harm
others to get little advantages for themselves, find them-

selves imprisoned in tiny, dark cells when they move to the Other Side. Therefore, live unselfishly! Be a blessing to others! If God has blessed you with wealth and abundance, with position and power, it is so that you may be a blessing to others. Receiving without giving makes a person full and proud and selfish. Give out the best in yourself, in God's name, for the good of others. The day on which I have not helped someone—a brother here or a sister there—to lift the load on the rough road of life is a lost day, indeed.

Let us come back to the picture on which each one of us will meditate today. In the moment of death, I stand in the radiant presence of God, the Being of Light, who looks at me with tender, understanding, love-filled eyes, and puts to me the question: "My child! What have you done with your life?" *My child! What have you done with your life?*

Remain silent for ten minutes.

By God's grace, the period of silence is now over. Now let us rub the palms of our hands together, place them softly on the eyelids, and gently, very gently, open the eyes.

Om shanti, shanti, shanti!

Self-Surrender Meditation

Let us, for a brief while, forget the world—its worries and vexations, its tensions and tribulations—and feel that we are in the presence of God. God is always with us: we are not always with God. Therefore, we need to practise the presence of God. Every time we find our thoughts straying away from God, let us bring the mind gently, lovingly, back into the Divine Presence.

Before beginning this meditation, let us offer a simple prayer:

> O Lord! May our senses be free from the
> drag of sense-objects. May our minds sit still
> in the Divine Presence, be illumined
> with the light of the Atman. May our
> entire being be filled with light. Light, light,
> light in front, light behind, light to the
> right, light to the left, light above, light
> below, light within, light all around. Light,
> light, light!

Now let us sit in a comfortable posture, so that we will not need to change it, for a period of about twenty-five minutes. Let us sit straight with the neck, the head, and the back in a straight line. And now let us take in three deep breaths. As you breathe deeply, be relaxed. Now begin.

(Pause)

Now let us utter the sacred word *Om* three times. Take in

a deep breath, and as you let it out utter the sacred syllable *Om.*

Begin. Take in a deep breath. *O…m* (pause). *O…m* (pause). *O…m.*

Now visualize Jesus standing, with arms outstretched, on the banks of the River Jordan. The flowing waters of the river symbolize the flux of things. In this world, everything keeps on changing; nothing abides. Everything is moving to its eternal drift. The Eternal alone does not change. Jesus is the symbol of the Eternal. He is the Divine Self seated in the heart of everyone.

Come back to Jesus standing, with arms outstretched, on the banks of the River Jordan. His open arms invite all pilgrims on the Path to come and receive His love and benedictions. Jesus does not belong to one sect, community, church. He belongs to all humanity. His message rings across the centuries: "Leave all things you have and come and follow Me."

By the side of Jesus is a lamb. The lamb symbolizes the New Testament and other world scriptures. Each lamb gives its own type of wool. But the wool of every lamb has the same quality of giving warmth. The inspiration of all scriptures is the same; the wisdom of all scriptures is one! In the New Testament are found the sayings of Jesus. Let us take up one of them, the saying in which the Lord declares: "Come unto Me, you that are weary and heavy-laden, and I shall give you rest!"

Let us meditate on those words. Let us enter into the depths of the meanings contained in the saying. Let us try to understand what it is to "come unto" Jesus. Let us say to Him, out of the very depths of our heart: "Lord! I have wandered much. I have wandered long. I have wandered far and wide. I come to You, weary and heavy-laden. I come to You as I am, full of faults and failings, frailties and imperfections. I come to You as I am. Accept me and make of me what You will. Make me, mould me, shape me, so that You are not ashamed of me. I shall not complain. I shall accept Your Will and rejoice in all the changing vicissitudes of life. In health and sickness, in prosperity and adversity, in praise and censure, in cold and heat, out of the very depths of my heart will come this one prayer, again and again: In sun and rain, in loss and gain, in pleasure and pain, Your Will be done! Your Will be done! In the acceptance of Your Will is the rest and true peace of the soul!"

Ten minutes of silence

Now rub the palms of your hands together and place them on your eyelids, and gently, very gently, open your eyes and look around you before you get up. Carry the spirit of the meditation with you into the activities of your day.

SUTRAS
(Thoughts for Meditation)

1

He who does My work, is devoted to Me, is void of attachment, and hath no hatred to any being—he cometh unto Me!

Bhagavad Gita

2

Dost thou still seek the pleasures of sex or stomach? Thou wilt not know Brahman, the Eternal God!

The Upanishads

3

If a man possessed the whole world, he would not be wealthy thereby, because it perishes and passes away.

Rabia

4

Though your life lasts a hundred years, you die like the short-lived man. The years swiftly pass!

Mahavira

5

With coarse food to eat, water to drink, and a bent arm for a pillow, happiness may still be found.

Confucius

6

Be in this world like a traveller, or like a passer-on, and reckon yourself as of the dead.

Muhammad

7

Which religion gives the greatest joy to God? That which giveth love and compassion to all creatures.

Vallabh Acharya

8

Seek and ye shall find!
Neglect and ye shall lose!

Mencius

9

Many a man by his babble shows that he is empty, indeed. But a few there be who show by their silence that they are divine.

Tauler

10

Forgiveness is the strength of the weak and ornament of the strong.

Chanakya

11

A bad thought is the most dangerous of thieves.

Chinese Saying

12

The beginnings of all things are small.

Cicero

13

Money spent on ourselves may be a millstone about the neck; spent on others it may give us wings like eagles.

R. D. Hitchcock

14

Loving-kindness is greater than laws; and the charities of life are more than ceremonies.

Talmud

15

Two are the qualities of him who is self-controlled:
1) forgiveness and 2) gentleness.

Rajarishi Yudhishthira

16

When you cannot find peace in yourself, it is useless to look for it elsewhere.

La Rochefoucauld

17

The highest wisdom is never to worry about the future but to resign ourselves entirely to His will.

Mahatma Gandhi

18

God is in thy heart, yet thou searchest for Him in the wilderness.

Guru Granth Sahib

19

Heaven and earth are impartial. They regard all creatures as sacred.

Lao Tse

20

The Self is dearer than a son, dearer than wealth, dearer than all else, and is the innermost.

Brihadaranyaka Upanishad

21

If a Jew breaks a leg, he should say: "Praised be God that I did not break both legs."

If he breaks both legs, he should say: "Praised be God that I did not break my neck."

Yiddish Proverb

22

Moral life is the backbone of the spiritual life. There cannot be any spiritual life without a moral life.

Swami Sivananda

23

Long for God alone. He may or may not meet you. But long only for Him.

Jamshed Nusserwanji

24

Our greatest glory is not in never failing, but in rising every time we fall.

Confucius

25

Prayer does not change God, but changes him who prays.

Søren Kierkegaard

26

Keep your mind pure in the battlefield of life.

Rig Veda

27

Pray as if everything depended on God, and work as if everything depended on man.

Author Unknown

28

Be humble and thy prayer will pierce through all the clouds and reach the Throne of God.

Sadhu Vaswani

29

Never think that God's delays are God's denials. Hold on, hold fast, hold out. Patience is genius.

Comte de Buffon

30

The secret of happiness is not in doing what one likes, but in liking what one has to do.

James Barrie

31

If thou wilt indeed live, learn first to die!

Tukaram

32

He who hath no check upon his tongue hath not truth in his heart.

Kabir

33

You will have to give an account of every careless word you utter.

Matthew 12:36

34

Be humble and gentle in your conversation, and of few words; and meddle not into other folks' matters.

William Penn

35

Wouldst thou win purity? Then cleanse thyself with these three: good thoughts, good words, good deeds.

Zoroaster

36

Turn thine eyes unto thyself and beware thou judge not the deeds of others!

Thomas à Kempis

37

The wise man does not teach by words but by deeds.

Lao Tse

38

Meditation on God is my food; His praise is my drink; and to bear witness to His Glory is my garment.

Junnuna Misri

39

Happy is the Muslim, for if good befalls him, he thanks God; and if evil befalls him, he praises God and bears his misfortune patiently.

Muhammad

40

Let's reform the world, shouts the social worker. Fine, agrees the saint, you reform yourself, I reform myself, and immediately the world is better.

Anonymous

41

He who hears the inner voice within him has no need to listen to outer words.

Jalalu'd Din Rumi

42

Every man feels instinctively that all the beautiful sentiments in the world weigh less than a single lovely action.

James Russell Lowell

43

Man was endowed with two ears and one tongue, that he may listen more than speak.

Abraham Hasdai

44

Time goes, you say? Ah no! Alas, Time stays, we go.

Austin Dobson

45

I am the Father of the whole universe, the Mother, the Creator, the Lord, the Friend.

Bhagavad Gita

46

The self cannot be gained by knowledge.

Katha Upanishad

47

If thou wilt know thyself, lose thy self, in love! And thou wilt find thyself.

Sadhu Vaswani

48

He that sinneth, sinneth unto himself.

He that is unjust, hurts himself, in that he makes himself worse than he was before.

Marcus Aurelius

49

It is not the knowing that is difficult, but the doing.

Shu King

50

All beings feel pleased by sweet speech; one should therefore talk sweet.

What does it cost to do so?

Chanakya

51

Naughty or good, I am Thy child. Sinner or saint, I am Thy child.

Paramahansa Yogananda

52

I am always with myself, and it is I who am my tormentor.

Leo Tolstoy

53

Three are the gateways of hell leading to the ruin of the soul: lust, wrath, and greed. Therefore, let man renounce these three.

Bhagavad Gita

54

We cannot be certain of living the next minute. But we are not content with even a million plans.

Kural

55

Everything is God. Good fortune is God; misfortune is God. Greet Him in everything and rest peacefully in bliss.

Swami Sivananda

56

All that a man bears for God's sake, God makes light and sweet for him.

Meister Eckhart

57

Allah is in the East and Allah is in the West; wherever you turn there is Allah's Face!

The Qur'an

58

The sages look alike on all—a learned Brahman, a cow, an elephant, a dog, or an outcast!

Bhagavad Gita

59

In every form behold the One Face of Beauty. To see aught else is a sin!

Sachal

60

However men approach Me, even so do I greet them as Mine own: For all the paths men take from any side are Mine, verily Mine!

Bhagavad Gita

61

If the Mussulman understood what the idol really was, he would know that there was true religion in idolatry.

Mahmud of Sabister

62

See ye what I behold? Verily, the Lord hath become the One-in-all, the All-in-one!

Ramakrishna

63

Blessed is the way of the Helpers. They are the companions of Christ!

H. Van Dyke

64

We gain only as we give.

Author Unknown

65

Men resemble the gods in nothing so much as in doing good to their fellow-creatures.

Cicero

66

The highest freedom consists in complete devotion to God. With God begin, with God complete, the day.

Author Unknown

67

Proceed on the axiom that all are godly, and everyone will behave as God if you behave as God toward them.

Swami Rama Tirtha

68

Half, if not two-thirds, of our ailings and diseases are the fruits of our imagination and fears.

H. P. Blavatsky

69

There are three things with which wisdom cannot exist: covetousness, licentiousness, and pride.

Welsh Triad

70

Lord Zoroaster showed two ways to conserve purity: control of temper and hard labour.

Jamshed Nusserwanji

71

All sins are committed in secrecy. The moment we realize that God witnesses even our thoughts we shall be free.

Mahatma Gandhi

72

That person will not enter paradise who hath one atom of pride in his heart.

Muhammad

73

Happiness does not consist in things but in thoughts.

Author Unknown

74

Prayer is conscious union with Cosmic Intelligence. Prayer is not supplication; it is Oneness.

Julia Seton Sears

75

Beware! Beware! Your actions will recoil on your own head!

Tseng Tze

76

There is one Instructor; there is no second different from Him. I speak concerning Him Who abides in the heart.

Anu Gita

77

Rabbi Eleazer said: "Repent one day before your death." Said his pupils: "Does man know when he would die?" He answered: "Then he surely must repent today, lest he die tomorrow."

Anonymous

78

Be doers of the word, and not merely hearers.

James 1:22

79

The way we rise in the scale of evolution is to raise others. The secret of achievement is self-effacement.

Sadhu Vaswani

80

He is not a perfect Muslim who eats his fill and lets his neighbour go hungry.

Muhammad

81

In all the world there is no such thing as a stranger.

Kurosumi Kyo

82

Behold the man who killeth not and who abstaineth from flesh-meat. All the world joineth hands and riseth to do him reverence.

Kural

83

The Sufi has no individual will. His will is merged in the Will of God; his will becomes the very Will of God.

Jami

84

True love means to give all that thou hast to Him whom thou lovest, so that nothing remains to thee of thine own.

Abu Abdallah Al Qurashi

85

When God loves a servant, He proves him by suffering.

Hudayfa B. Husayl Al-Yaman

86

When the heart weeps for what it has lost, the spirit laughs for what it has found.

Abu Sulayman

87

In this broad, boundless sea of life Thou art my Boat. How can I cross without Thee, Beloved?

Mira

88

My rule of life: Love God and serve the Brotherhood!

Author Unknown

89

It is better in prayer to have a heart without words, than words without a heart.

Mahatma Gandhi

90

When obstacles and trials seem like prison walls to me, I do the little I can do, and leave the rest to Thee.

F. W. Faber

91

Thou art not safe until thou hast surrendered thyself wholly to the Lord!

Sadhu Vaswani

92

O Lord! So bless me that, in all the changing vicissitudes of life, I may never lose sight of thee.

J. P.

93

In prayer what is essential is not words but the deep silence of communion.

J. P.

94

God's plan is perfect, and whatever happens is for the best.

J.P

95

Wondrous are the fruits of silence. He who tastes them, for him there is nothing more to be learned.

J. P.

96

In all situations of life, keep calm. The inner balance is essential to spiritual progress.

J. P.

97

Harmonious living is more important than doing deeds of service.

J. P.

98

There is no problem that cannot be solved. In God is the solution to all problems.

J. P.

99

You may have a number of appointments to keep every day. Never forget to keep your appointment with God!

J. P.

100

Which is the quickest—and easiest—way to God?
The way of Love!

J. P.

ABOUT THE AUTHOR

J. P. Vaswani was born on August 2, 1918, at Hyderabad Sind, India. He was a fellow at the D. J. Sind College, Karachi, when he gave up a bright academic future to follow his guru, his uncle Sadhu Vaswani—a mystic, philosopher, humanitarian, and educator. J. P. Vaswani has followed in his uncle's footsteps, modelling his life according to the Bhagavad Gita and Jesus' Sermon on the Mount. His message is one of reverence and love for all of life. He is also widely hailed as an inspirational speaker in India, and he has spoken at the Dag Hammarskjöld Auditorium of the United Nations and at a reception arranged for him at the English House of Commons.

J. P. Vaswani has published thirty books in English, among them *From Hell to Heaven, The Good You Do Returns!* and *Daily Appointment with God,* and several more in Sindhi.

J. P. Vaswani travels extensively and says that the earth is his country and to do good is his religion.

*Other books on prayer and meditation
published by Burns & Oates*

NO MAN IS AN ISLAND
Thomas Merton

This is a book about real things that are so solid we tend to ignore them. It proclaims the spiritual life as the life of our actual selves, as the really real life. It asserts and insists with firmness (yet with a sweet profundity that is never in the least cloying) the great truth that life must have a meaning. Thomas Merton shows that meaning as arising in the pursuit of our common destiny but as something we each have to work out for ourselves, in our own unique way, in fear and trembling.

This is a book about aspiration, asceticism and above all sacrifice—of oneself and of one's domination of self. It is about the choice between life and death, our last and most important decision.

"The author's most valuable achievement so far; it should find its place among the enduring works of Christian spirituality" *Commonweal*

"A stimulating and strengthening experience. What he writes is the issue of genuinely personal thought and suggestive of a deeper than merely intellectual experience" *The Month*

"By far the best thing he has done. It stands in a class by itself and deserves to hold a place among the great classics of the spiritual life ... This is a book by a mature monk who has been through the crucible and come out of it with wider horizons, a more balanced outlook and a more profound wisdom. It is the book of a monk who has learned much in the 'school of the love of God' and is concerned to pass on to others the fruit of his contemplation ... The author covers all the salient aspects of the spiritual life, and there is none that he does not illuminate" *The Tablet*

THE WAY OF CHUANG-TZU
Thomas Merton

Thomas Merton describes this, his personal favourite of his books, as "not attempts at faithful reproduction but ventures in personal and spiritual interpretation." As free, interpretative readings, they are very much Merton's own, the result of five years of reading, study and meditation.

Chuang Tzu, the most spiritual of the classic Chinese philosophers, is the chief historical spokesman for Taoism. Through his writings and those of other Taoist sages, Indian Buddhism was transformed in China into what we now know by its Japanese name—Zen.

The Chinese sage abounds in wit, paradox, satire and shattering insight into the true ground of being. Merton here brings a vivid, modern idiom to the timeless wisdom of Tao.

CONJECTURES OF A GUILTY BYSTANDER
Thomas Merton

"Maybe the best way to characterize this book is to say that it consists of a series of sketches and meditations, some poetic and literary, other historical and even theological, fitted together in a spontaneous, informal philosophic scheme in such a way that they react upon each other. The total result is a personal and monastic meditation, a testimony of Christian reflection ... a confrontation of twentieth-century questions in the light of a monastic commitment, which inevitably makes one something of a 'bystander'"

Based on the journals Merton kept from 1956 to late 1965, three years before his tragic accidental death in 1968, this series of comments on questions of that time and others very much reflects the author's view of the Second Vatican Council.

Such reflections are interspersed with views on writers as diverse as Camus, Gandhi, Bonhoeffer, Teilhard de Chardin, and many others. Light relief is provided by sparkling and humorous anecdotes of life in the monastery.